MW00934309

THIS BOOK BELONGS TO

____

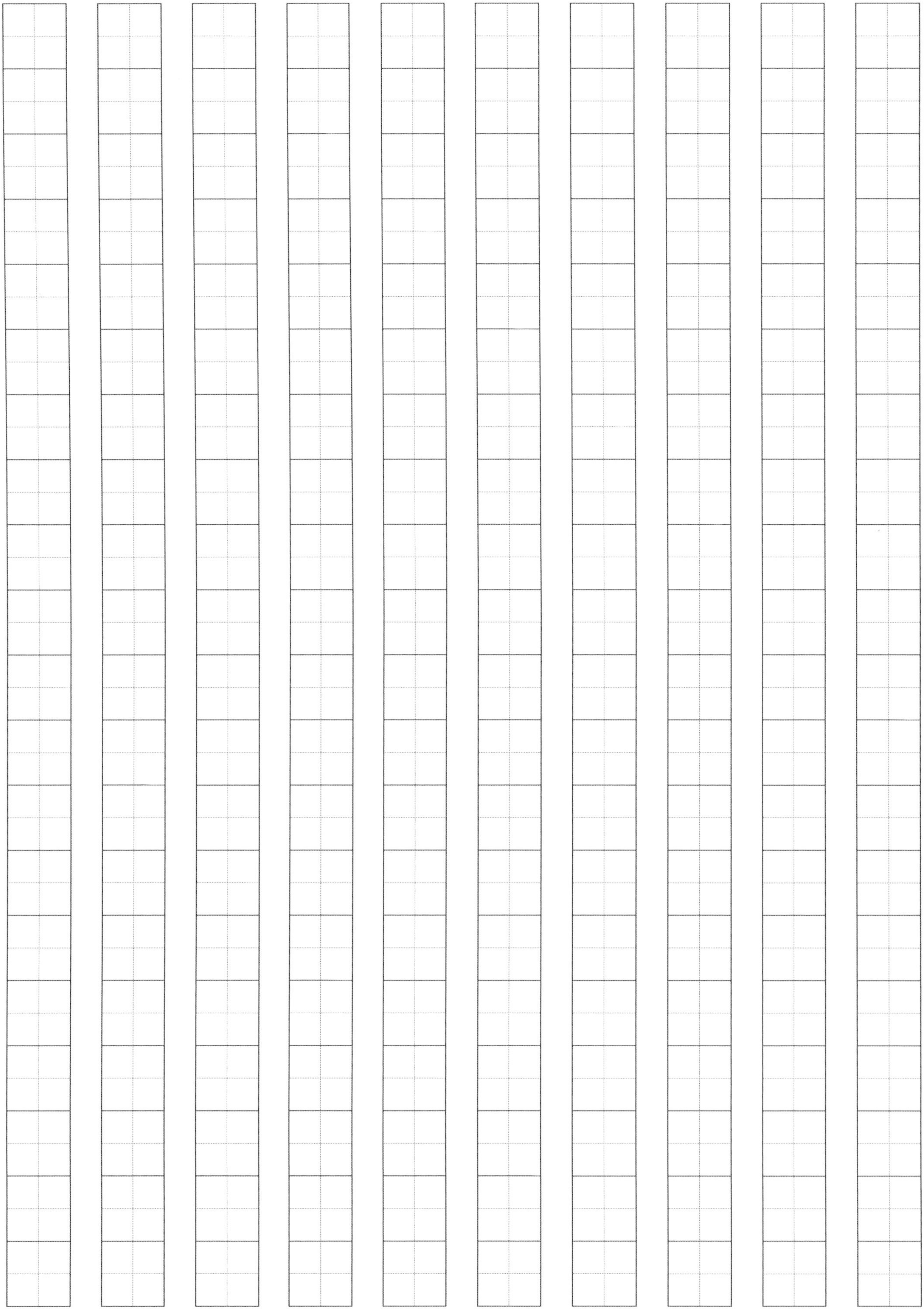

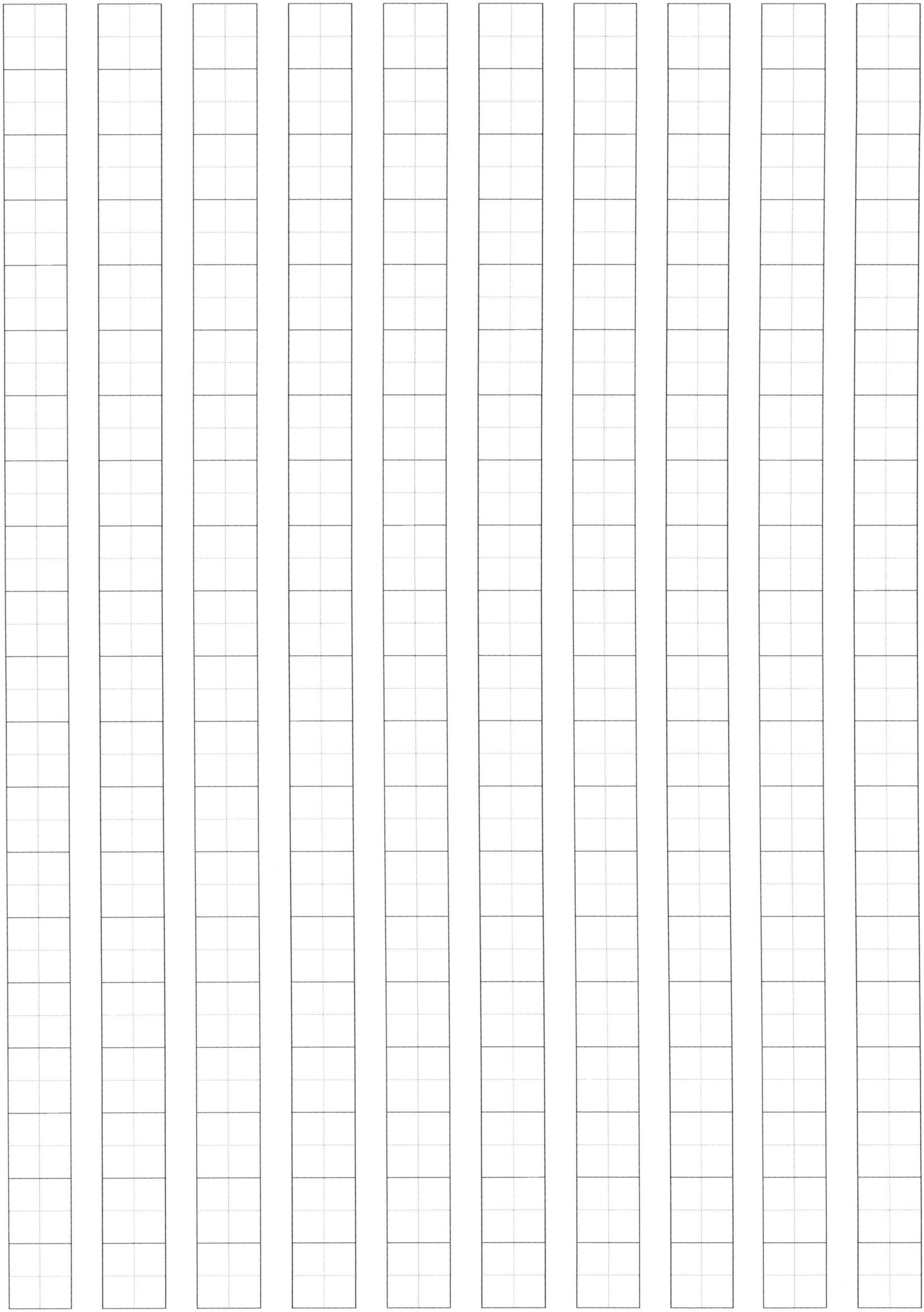

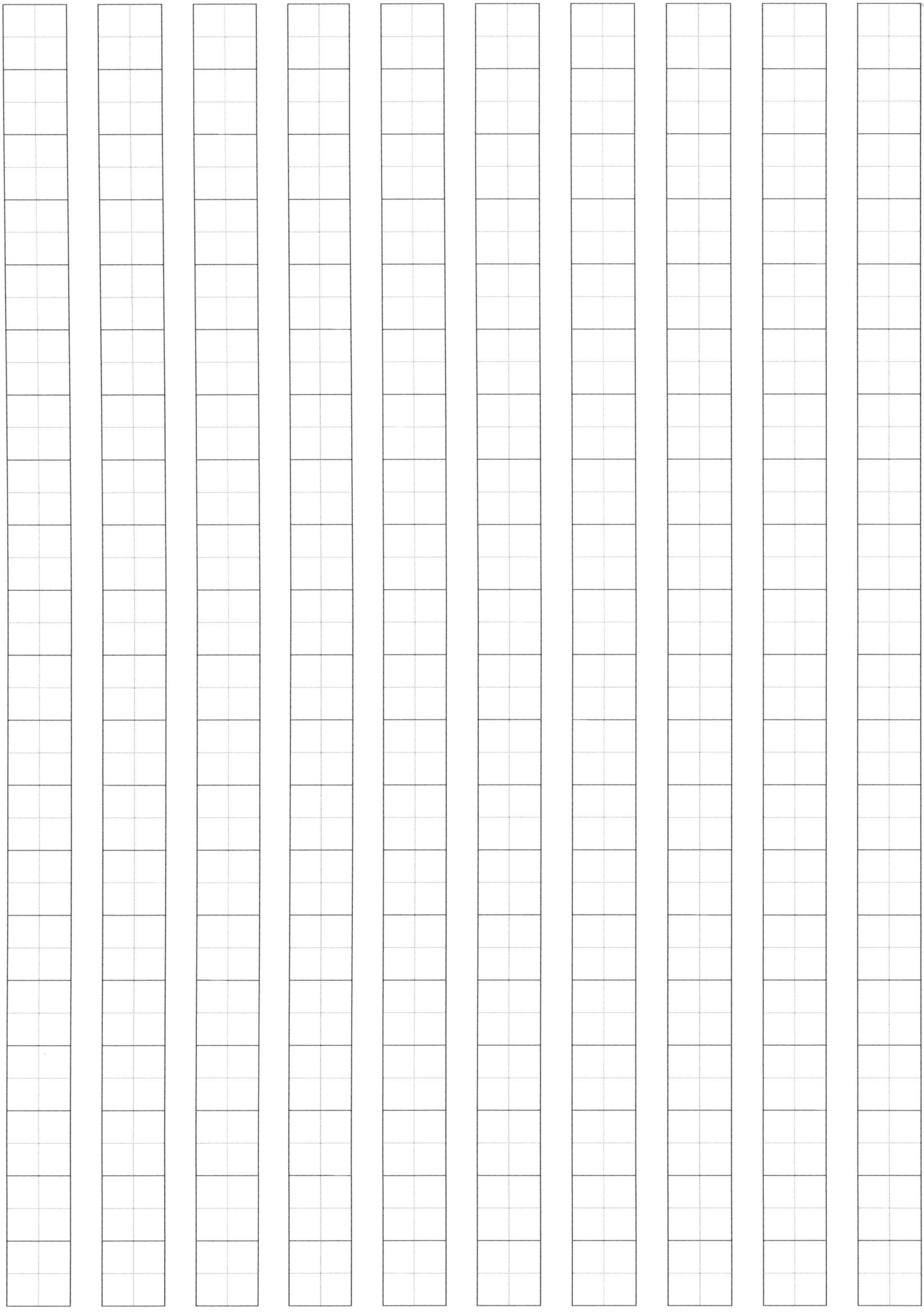

Made in the USA
San Bernardino, CA
10 May 2020

71157882R00058